Since 1888, *National Geographic* magazine has provided its readers a wealth of information and helped us understand the world in which we live. Insightful articles, supported by gorgeous photography and impeccable research, bring the mission of the National Geographic Society front and center: to inspire people to care about the planet. The *Explore* series delivers *National Geographic* to you in the same spirit. Each of the books in this series presents the best articles on popular and relevant topics in an accessible format. In addition, each book highlights the work of National Geographic Explorers, photographers, and writers. Explore the world of *National Geographic*. You will be inspired.

ON THE COVER
Chinstrap penguins on a blue iceberg in the South Sandwich Islands of Antarctica

ANTARCTICA

For centuries European explorers searched for the gigantic continent in the middle of the icy southern waters. Antarctica was the last of the seven continents to be discovered, and it did not reveal itself all at once. Each voyage of discovery led to additional questions, which explorers would try to answer on future expeditions. Were the sailors looking at a continent, or had they spotted portions of an island chain? Was the landmass they encountered inhabitable? Did it hold valuable minerals and wildlife? Through the centuries, explorers risked their lives and their health under the harsh conditions at the frozen extreme of the planet for answers to these and other questions. Some earned fame, admiration, wealth, and scientific insight. Others tragically died.

People who work in Antarctica today are dedicated to peaceful international cooperation in the search for scientific knowledge, including many studies on climate change. The continent is a unique laboratory for this work because of its isolation from large populations, its cold, dry climate, and the scientific talent that has gathered there.

Perhaps you'll begin reading this book, as the explorers began, with an image of Antarctica as gigantic, white, cold, and empty. As you read, your picture will transform with color and detail from history, geography, biology, astronomy, climate studies, and photography. Antarctica and the waters that surround it are both lively and rapidly changing.

Today it is easy to get real-time information about Antarctica when you want it. Online, for example, you'll find very old, fanciful maps, recent photographic blogs created by tourists, and videos of daily life at the Amundsen-Scott station at the South Pole. There is even a series of cartoons from the *Antarctic Sun,* the daily newspaper of the southern continent. Just as all lines of longitude meet at the South Pole, numerous lines of curiosity meet there too.

Chinstrap penguins thrive on Antarctica's rocky shores.

Discovering

BY JON BOWERMASTER
Adapted from "The Story of Antarctic
Exploration," by Jon Bowermaster, on
jonbowermaster.com, 2008

AN EXTREME LAND
Explorers slip between icebergs near
Pleneau Island, off Antarctica. This icy
sea has defied sailors for centuries.

Antarctica

From the start, Antarctic exploration has been driven by scientific discovery, desire for profits, quests for adventure, and sheer curiosity. The continent and its surrounding waters have felt the effects of human activity for centuries.

The Race to the South Pole

As early as the 1500s, seafaring explorers believed there was a great continent far to the south of the known world. For centuries, however, nobody succeeded in spotting Antarctica. Sailors did, however, see large numbers of seals and whales in the oceans far to the south, and these reports spawned human greed. By the late 1700s, hunters were headed south. Between 1784 and 1822, millions of sealskins were taken from the islands that had been discovered. This drove the seal population there nearly to extinction. As others traveled further south and sighted more seals, the hunters followed and the slaughter continued.

The explorers who pushed south were seeking to discover new lands and chart the area. Captain Thaddeus von Bellingshausen commanded an Antarctic expedition funded by Russia. His progress to the south was stopped by a massive, continental **ice shelf** on January 16, 1820. This ice shelf was the first sighting of the continent of Antarctica by human eyes. The end of the 1800s and beginning of the 1900s saw the greatest upsurge in Antarctic exploration to date. The reason for this flurry of activity was a shift away from profit toward science—and national pride.

In 1901, Robert Scott's first expedition to Antarctica left England aboard the ship *Discovery*. One of Scott's main goals was to reach the South Pole. Once Scott set up winter camp, *Discovery* promptly became frozen into the ice. She stayed that way for the next two years. Scott and his men made good use of the time. On numerous exploratory **sledge** trips from camp, the men busied themselves discovering, naming, and mapping out new territory and geographic landmarks. They attempted to reach the South Pole but harsh conditions, inadequate diet, and slow progress finally forced them to turn around.

The final assault on the South Pole is a story both of brilliant success and desperate failure. It began in January 1911. Roald Amundsen of Norway arrived at the Bay of Whales. Robert Scott, leading his second expedition, arrived at Cape Evans, Ross Island. Both built substantial camps and settled in for the winter.

On October 20th, which falls during spring in the Southern Hemisphere, Amundsen and four others set out for the pole with sledges and dog teams. On December 14, 1911, the team succeeded and became the first to reach the geographic South Pole.

Robert Scott and four others began their attempt on the South Pole on November 1, 1911. Where Amundsen had used sled dogs, Scott's party hauled their own sledges over rough snow and treacherous glaciers. The going was slow and difficult. Finally, on January 17, 1912, they reached the pole, only to find Amundsen's tent and a Norwegian flag waiting for them. The sight destroyed their morale. Short of food and pinned in their tent several times by storms, all five died on the return trip. You can read more about Amundsen and Scott's expeditions later in this book, beginning on page 18.

The Shackleton Expedition

The most incredible survival story in Antarctic history is that of the expedition led by legendary explorer Ernest Shackleton. This expedition left England in the ship *Endurance* on August 8, 1914. Shackleton's plan was to cross the continent from the Weddell Sea to the Ross Sea. However, before it ever reached Antarctica, the *Endurance* became trapped in the **pack ice** and remained imprisoned through the winter. Ultimately, the ship was crushed to pieces by the ice and sank on November 21, 1915.

ICEBOUND
Ernest Shackleton's ship, the *Endurance*, is trapped in the relentless grip of the pack ice off Antarctica in 1915.

Shackleton and his men dragged and rowed their lifeboats over the ice and through the occasional **lead** until they made it to Elephant Island. From there, Shackleton and five others set out in a 20-foot boat to cross 800 miles of the stormiest seas in the world. After 15 grueling days, they arrived at the southern shore of South Georgia Island. Rough seas delayed their landing for two days. Shackleton and two others then climbed across the mountainous island (with no food, water, or shelter) to reach the whaling station at Stromness Bay.

Meanwhile, the 22 men left on Elephant Island survived by using upturned boats as shelters. Finally, after several unsuccessful attempts, Shackleton returned in the Chilean trawler *Yelcho* to rescue the nearly starved men 105 days after they had arrived.

Technology, Hunting, and Exploration

During the early 1800s, whalers were looking for additional stocks of the rapidly disappearing southern right whales. They found only rorquals (a type of fast-swimming whale) for which their rowboats were no match, so they fell back on taking fur and elephant seals. By 1825, most of the seals had been wiped out.

Whaling technology had improved by the early 20th century. Faster catcher boats and explosive harpoons finally permitted the taking of rorquals. The industry was re-established in Antarctic waters in 1904.

Attempts were made to conserve the whales, especially the younger ones. Nonetheless, tens of thousands of whales were killed, many of them immature. By 1965, the industry was in decline, having committed the same error and suffered the same fate as the sealing industry before it.

In the 20th century, technology was also changing Antarctic exploration with more powerful engines, steel-hulled ships, airplanes, and radios. One pioneer during this period was Admiral Richard Byrd of the United States. Byrd and his team reached the Ross Ice Shelf on December 25, 1928. His goal was to fly over the South Pole. After establishing his Little America camp, Byrd made his first flight on January 15, 1929. The next **austral** summer, Byrd and three others took off and headed south. After a harrowing climb over the Transantarctic Mountains, Byrd and his crew became the first to fly over the South Pole.

International Cooperation

As more and more governments began to realize the potential strategic, economic, and scientific importance of the last continent, they began to lay claim to vast tracts of Antarctic land.

The oldest continuously occupied station in Antarctica is the weather station on Laurie Island in the South Orkneys. It has belonged to Argentina since 1904. However, the first formal claim over Antarctic territory was made by Great Britain in 1908. New Zealand, France, Australia, Norway, and Chile also made claims to various parts of the continent. The United States pursued no claims of its own but it established the U.S. Antarctic Service in 1939. From that moment on, the U.S. government assumed almost complete control of American Antarctic exploration.

By the late 1940s, countries were building permanent bases, and the scramble to occupy the continent was on. Much of the base construction was to support Antarctic research. As winter 1956 closed in, there were 29 separate parties in Antarctica from 7 countries.

In 1959, countries that had claimed land on the continent signed the Antarctic Treaty. This treaty set Antarctica aside for peaceful, scientific purposes and placed all territorial claims on hold.

Unlike the political success of the treaty, our environmental record in Antarctica has not been good. Humans have affected the continent through **exploitation**, pollution, and disturbance. Seals were hunted almost to extinction. Whale stocks were reduced to small fractions of their estimated original populations. People on early expeditions to Antarctica simply tossed their garbage overboard. Whalers left whole stations abandoned and crumbling. Technology began to produce materials such as gasoline and plastic that had never existed

ANTARCTICA TODAY
Adélie penguins cluster near the Argentina Research Station. Modern-day
visitors and explorers strive to leave Antarctic wildlife untouched.

in nature. In the cold and dry Antarctic environment, where unpainted wood can last for centuries, synthetic products can be expected to persist essentially forever.

Within the last few years, however, government agencies involved in Antarctic research have taken steps to protect the environment. Most of Antarctica's biological resources are now protected to some degree. Only a certain level of whaling is permitted for scientific purposes. Similarly, current agreements prohibit mining activity until at least 2041. To reduce the impact of human visitors, it is now the practice to remove waste from the continent. Through cooperation, the international community is now making efforts to halt the damage to Antarctica's fragile ecosystem.

THINK ABOUT IT! ||||||||||||||||||||||||||||||||

1 **Make Generalizations** What motivates people to discover and explore new places? Use details from this article to support your ideas.

2 **Analyze Cause and Effect** What made it possible for humans to venture deeper into Antarctica and exploit its resources?

3 **Form and Support Opinions** Do you expect that the treaties in place to protect Antarctic wildlife will succeed? Why or why not?

BACKGROUND & VOCABULARY

austral *adj.* (AW-struhl) relating to the Southern Hemisphere

exploitation *n.* (ehks-ploy-TAY-shuhn) the act of making use of a resource for one's own advantage

ice shelf *n.* the thick ice formed by glaciers extending out over the ocean at the edge of a continent

lead *n.* (LEED) a passage of open water through the ice pack

pack ice *n.* a wide area of ice floating on the ocean's surface

sledge *n.* (SLEHJ) a vehicle on runners, used to pull loads over ice and snow

9

Antarctica's
Life

People who live there for any length of time call Antarctica "the ice," appropriate for a continent with a two-mile-thick cap of it. Despite the harsh conditions, though, diverse populations of wildlife survive here. Animals as small as two-inch krill and as large as 100-foot-long blue whales thrive in the waters around Antarctica. Many species of birds—including several different kinds of penguins—and seals live on both land and in water. Scientists from all over the world gather at research stations to study the wildlife, the environment, and the effects of changing climate.

Maximum extent of sea ice

Krill concentra

South Sandwich Is.

Neum

South Georgia

Krill concentrations

Minimum extent of sea ice

Halley U.K.

Scotia Sea

South Orkney Is.

Belgrano II Argentina

Weddell Sea

SOUTH ATLANTIC OCEAN

South Shetland Is.
South Korea King Sejong
King George I.
Chile Presidente Eduardo Frei
Livingston I.
Deception I.
Port Lockroy (Historic site)

Paulet I.
Hope Bay
Esperanza Argentina

Ronne Ice Shelf

Antarctic Peninsula

Falkland Is. U.K.

60°

Humble I.
Rothera

Terra Firma Is.

Ellsworth Land

Vinson Massif 16,067 ft 4,897 m

Buenos Aires
SOUTH AMERICA

Cape Horn

Drake Passage

Bellingshausen Sea

W

ANTA

ARGENTINA

Tierra del Fuego

Punta Arenas

Krill concentrations

CHILE

SOUTH PACIFIC OCEAN

Amundsen Sea

ANTARCTIC CIRCLE

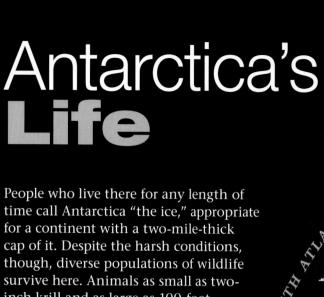

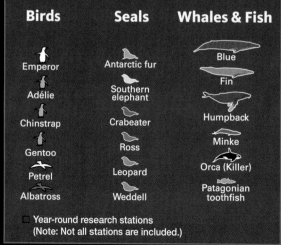

Birds	Seals	Whales & Fish
Emperor	Antarctic fur	Blue
Adélie	Southern elephant	Fin
Chinstrap	Crabeater	Humpback
Gentoo	Ross	Minke
Petrel	Leopard	Orca (Killer)
Albatross	Weddell	Patagonian toothfish

☐ Year-round research stations
(Note: Not all stations are included.)

AE IV
Africa

Maitri
India

ovolazarevskaya
Russia

Syowa
Japan

Molodezhnaya
Russia

Mawson
Australia

Krill
concentrations

ANTARCTIC CIRCLE

30° E

60°

Kerguelen Is.
France

Heard I.
Australia

INDIAN OCEAN

China Zhongshan
Russia Progress

Australia Davis

EAST

ANTARCTICA

90°

Mirnyy
Russia

Davis
Sea

Amundsen-Scott
South Pole U.S.
9,301 ft
2,835 m

South Pole

Vostok
Russia

Maximum
extent of
sea ice

Casey
Australia

ctic

ANTARCTICA

Beardmore
Glacier

Mt. Henderson
8,727 ft
2,660 m

Concordia
(Seasonal research station)
France and Italy

120°

Ross
Ice Shelf

Mountains

Darwin Glacier

Scott Base
New Zealand

McMurdo
U.S.

Minimum
extent of
sea ice

Mt. Erebus
12,448 ft
3,794 m

Cape Evans

Ross I.

Dumont d'Urville
France

Cape
Crozier

Mt. Melbourne
8,963 ft
2,732 m

★ 2001 South
Magnetic
Pole

Ross
Sea

180°

150° W

Krill
concentrations

Balleny Is.

AUSTRALIA

Scale varies in this perspective.

Melbourne

Escape Velocity

BY GLENN HODGES
Adapted from "Escape Velocity," by Glenn Hodges,
in *National Geographic*, November 2012

For Antarctica's emperor penguins, it's survival of the swiftest. Penguins are famous for their spectacular leaps from the water. Only recently have scientists discovered the blend of feathers and physics that enables these flightless birds to soar

Penguin Physics

Marine biologist Roger Hughes has never seen emperor penguins in the wild. But when he saw them in a documentary, he had an insight that would lead to a surprising discovery. The penguins were rocketing through the sea with trails of bubbles in their wakes. Hughes had recently been talking with his wife about the **lubricating** properties of new competitive swimsuits. He wondered: Maybe those bubbles help penguins swim faster.

Hughes is at Bangor University in north Wales, Great Britain. He bounced his hypothesis off his friend John Davenport, a marine biologist at University College Cork in Ireland. Davenport studies the relationship between animals' body structures and their movements. "Roger thought I'd have the answer straightaway," says Davenport. But he wasn't able to tell Hughes what the bubbles did. It turns out no one else knew either. The two men combed the scientific literature; they found that the phenomenon had never even been studied. So they decided to do it themselves.

With the help of Poul Larsen, a mechanical engineer at the Technical University of Denmark, they analyzed hours of underwater footage. They discovered the penguins were doing something that engineers had long tried to accomplish with boats and

AIR TIME
Before heading for land, penguins spend time at the surface loading their feathers with air.

torpedoes. They were using air as a lubricant to cut their **drag** and increase their speed.

When an emperor penguin swims through the water, it is slowed by the **friction** between its body and the water. This keeps its maximum speed somewhere between four to nine feet a second. But in short bursts the penguin can double or even triple its speed. It does so by releasing air from its feathers in the form of tiny bubbles. The bubbles reduce the density of the water around the penguin's body. The lower density of the water reduces the drag of friction on the penguin's body, thus enabling it to reach speeds that would otherwise be impossible.

LEAPING TO SAFETY
To get out of the water a penguin may have to clear several feet of ice—and any leopard seals lurking in hope of a meal.

MOUTHS TO FEED
Hungry chicks rely on
adult penguins to bring
food from the sea
several miles away.

The key to this ability is in the penguin's feathers. Most birds have rows of feathers with rows of bare skin between them. Emperor penguins have a dense, uniform coat of oil-infused feathers. Furthermore, they have precise muscular control over these feathers. Like other birds, emperors have the capacity to fluff their feathers with air in order to insulate their bodies from the cold. Emperors also have the ability to compress their feathers and release air at will. The pores in their feathers are just 20 microns in diameter, less than half the width of a human hair. Because the pores are so small, the air is released as microbubbles that are ideal for lubrication.

Lifesaving Speed

Penguins are in the greatest danger from one of their predators, leopard seals, when they enter the water. Penguins sometimes linger at the edge of an ice hole for hours, waiting for one bold bird to plunge in.

When they are leaving the water, however, the microbubble technique gives penguins an advantage in avoiding predators. Penguins hunt at sea to get food for their chicks. After the hunt, adult penguins spend time at the surface of the water loading their **plumage** with air. With their dense coat of fine-pored feathers emperor penguins can hold air in their plumage indefinitely. As they approach land, they'll dive deep, gather speed, force out the microbubbles, and rocket toward their exit hole. They clear several feet of ice and once more elude the waiting leopard seals.

Once safely back on land, the penguins look awkward and clumsy to human eyes as they move off with their slow, waddling gait. It will take water and just enough air to turn them once again into creatures of grace and stunning speed.

THINK ABOUT IT! ||||||||||||||||||||||||||||||||||||||||||||||||||||||||||||||||

1 **Find Main Ideas and Details** How do penguins reduce drag and friction when swimming?

2 **Sequence Events** Describe the process by which penguins can rapidly increase their speed when leaving the water.

BACKGROUND & VOCABULARY

drag *n.* the force exerted on a moving object by the air or water that surrounds it, slowing it down

friction *n.* (FRIHK-shuhn) the force that resists the motion of two objects that are touching and moving against each other

lubricating *adj.* (LOO-brih-kayt-ing) making it easier for two objects in contact to move against each other; reducing friction

plumage *n.* (PLOO-mihj) a bird's feathers

Amundsen:

The Man Who Took the Prize

BY CAROLINE ALEXANDER

Adapted from "The Man Who Took the Prize," by Caroline Alexander,
in *National Geographic*, September 2011

POLAR TRAVELERS
The Amundsen expedition relied on sled dogs to
cross Antarctica's dangerous, icebound terrain.

The Race for the Pole

The year was 1911, and the writer of this diary entry was Norwegian explorer Roald Amundsen. He was several days' march from his base camp at Bay of Whales, Antarctica, headed to the South Pole. He had decided to turn around.

Amundsen had become famous five years earlier for being the first to sail the Arctic's Northwest Passage. Explorers had been looking for this northern sea route from the Atlantic to the Pacific for centuries. Now Amundsen was at the opposite end of the world, aiming for the South Pole. It was the most prestigious prize the world of exploration still offered.

Amundsen was methodical and careful, but he was also a man of great ambition. All explorers who risk their lives in wild places are driven by dangerous dreams and impulses. Amundsen's greatness is not that he lacked such driving forces but that he mastered them. After turning around, he wrote, "To risk men and animals by continuing stubbornly once we have set off, is something I couldn't consider."

Roald Amundsen was well prepared for his South Pole venture. He was born in 1872 into a seafaring family. At 25, he sailed as member of a scientific expedition to the Antarctic. When the expedition's ship, the *Belgica*, became stuck in pack ice, the crew had to remain there all winter. They were the first humans to overwinter in the Antarctic. The crew members were discouraged and sick. The company was held together by the ship's surgeon, Frederick Cook, and by Amundsen.

Later, during his search for the Northwest Passage, Amundsen lived and worked over three winters in the Arctic. He came to know the Netsilik Eskimos and their superb adaptation to the Arctic world. Amundsen was not the first European explorer to learn from **indigenous** people. The great polar explorer Fridtjof Nansen and others had learned how to dress, travel, and eat from Norway's northern Sami people.

Now Amundsen supplemented that wisdom with survival tools he had studied and experienced firsthand: loose reindeer skin clothing that provided warmth and ventilation, fur boots, dogsleds, snowshoes, ice caves, igloos. Finally, Amundsen and his crew navigated a passage through the islands, shallows, and ice of Canada's Arctic **archipelago** to the Beaufort and then the Bering Sea—a historic first.

"The North-West Passage was done," Amundsen wrote of the event in his diary on August 26, 1905. "My boyhood dream—at that moment it was accomplished. A strange feeling welled up in my throat; I was somewhat overstrained and worn—it was a weakness in me—but I felt tears in my eyes."

Unknown Territory

When Roald Amundsen set up his base camp in Antarctica's Bay of Whales in January 1911, he was 38 years old and a seasoned polar veteran. He was in wholly unknown territory, but he was also in a familiar landscape of snow and ice. Amundsen and his men used the months preceding the polar journey to lay down **depots** of supplies. They subjected every article of food, clothing, and equipment to careful inspection and improvement.

Winning the South Pole, however, was not to be taken for granted. Also heading south was a British expedition. It was commanded by Captain Robert Falcon Scott. Amundsen was tormented by the possibility that Scott might beat him. For that reason, he started out before the polar springtime, when the weather would be more manageable, and was forced to turn back to his base camp. He lost valuable dogs as a result of his false start, and his men suffered frostbite that would take a month to heal.

Scott established his base camp on Ross Island in McMurdo Sound, the starting point of the two previous British expeditions. Scott himself had led one of them and Ernest Shackleton the other. Scott followed Shackleton's route. Amundsen's starting point positioned him a little closer to the pole—but committed him to striking out on an entirely new route over unknown terrain.

One dramatic difference between the two expeditions was how they pulled their supplies. Amundsen relied on dog teams to pull the sledges that carried his supplies. For Scott, dogs took away the "glory" of **sledging**. The ideal of "unaided" exploration was men hauling their own supplies. He was willing to try motor sledges, but these broke down. Scott also brought ponies, which required bulky feed and close care and sank up to their knees in snow. In contrast, Amundsen's faith in dogs grew with their use. "Today we have had a lot of loose snow although it doesn't affect our dogs," he wrote in his diary.

The teams also differed in their dress for the cold. The British team wore wool clothing and windproof tunics for hauling sledges. But survival required better. "I will call any expedition . . . without fur clothing, inadequately equipped," Amundsen noted.

Amundsen's journey to the pole was more than 800 miles. It began at last on October 20th, with Amundsen and his four companions on skis. They followed four loaded sledges; each one weighed 880 pounds and was pulled by 13 dogs. The terrain was **treacherous** and the weather dangerously unpredictable. Yet without any major accident, the Norwegians reached their goal on schedule. "And so at last we reached our destination," Amundsen wrote in his diary on December 14, 1911, "and planted our flag on the geographical South Pole. . . . Thank God!"

Scott's five-man party arrived 34 days later, having encountered the Norwegians' tracks in the final miles. Defeated, they understood that their labor had been, in Scott's words, "without the reward of priority."

On the return trip, Amundsen's men abandoned extra supplies. Ironically, some of these would be gratefully collected by Scott's party. Even so, Scott and his men died on the return journey.

Early on January 26, 1912, Amundsen and his team returned to their base camp. "Good morning, my dear Lindstrøm," he greeted his startled cook. "Have you any coffee for us?"

OUTFITTED FOR THE COLD
The British team (Robert Falcon Scott at center) poses for a photo in their outdoor gear. Scott and four others from the team made the push for the pole and died on the return trip.

Success and Failure

The contrast between what has been called Amundsen's "business-like" operation and Scott's "first-rate tragedy" highlights issues that still concern adventurers and explorers today. Amundsen used dogs; Scott ponies and motor sledges. Amundsen traveled by ski, a skill at which he and his men were adept; Scott never learned to ski well, so he and his men trudged, pulling their own sledges. Amundsen deposited three times the supplies Scott did; Scott starved and suffered **scurvy**.

The contrast between Amundsen and Scott is not about details of management. It is about broad outlooks—those of the professional and of the amateur. "In Norway there is *very* little tolerance for failure in expeditions," one historian says. "You go and you come back whole." The British, in contrast, emphasized the struggle; they believed that character, not skill, would win out and that death was heroic. That view would be judged irresponsible today.

Amundsen enjoyed celebrity until the end of his life. However, he never achieved financial security. In the 1920s, searching for new prizes, Amundsen turned to aviation. In 1926 he commanded the airship *Norge*, flown by Italian pilot Umberto Nobile, for the first successful crossing of the Arctic by air. Daring as these later adventures were, Amundsen participated more as passenger than leader. Short of money, he had become embittered, lashing out at old allies. Yet in May 1928, when Nobile's airplane went missing over the Arctic, Amundsen quickly joined the rescue effort. He boarded a rescue plane in

AT THE POLE
After planting the Norwegian flag at the South Pole, Amundsen and his team spent three days taking photos and measurements.

Tromsø, Norway, far to the north. The air was still, which often meant summer fog and poor visibility to the north. The plane was seen for the last time passing over the mountainous land along the coast. It was summer, and the land was green, but Amundsen was heading north, toward the ice. He was never seen again.

THINK ABOUT IT!

1 **Analyze Cause and Effect** How did Amundsen's early life prepare him for his Antarctic success?

2 **Analyze Visuals** How do the photos on pages 18 and 20 underscore the differences between the Amundsen and Scott expeditions?

3 **Make Inferences** Why might Scott's method of exploration be avoided today?

BACKGROUND & VOCABULARY

archipelago *n.* (ahr-kuh-PEHL-uh-goh) a large group of islands

depot *n.* (DEE-poh) a deposit of food and supplies laid out ahead of the journey

indigenous *adj.* (ihn-DIHJ-uh-nuhs) originally living in an area; native

scurvy *n.* (SKUR-vee) a disease caused by a lack of vitamin C

sledging *n.* (SLEHJ-ing) the act of pulling a sledge, a vehicle with runners used to pull loads over ice and snow

treacherous *adj.* (TREH-chur-uhs) dangerous

EXPLORER'S JOURNAL
with Jon Bowermaster

Adapted from "The White Continent Heats Up," by
Jon Bowermaster, in *National Geographic Adventure*,
November 2008

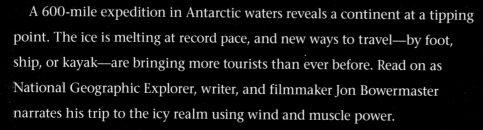

A 600-mile expedition in Antarctic waters reveals a continent at a tipping
point. The ice is melting at record pace, and new ways to travel—by foot,
ship, or kayak—are bringing more tourists than ever before. Read on as
National Geographic Explorer, writer, and filmmaker Jon Bowermaster
narrates his trip to the icy realm using wind and muscle power.

^ THE JOURNEY BEGINS
Jon Bowermaster
stands on the deck of
the *Pelagic Australis*,
bound for Antarctic
shores.

The White Continent Heats Up

Three days after leaving the southernmost yacht club in the world—in Puerto Williams, Chile—we begin our hunt for icebergs. About 200 miles from Antarctica's mainland, we're surrounded by black, 12-foot waves; we spy our first iceberg and float by quietly, respectfully. It is easily a hundred feet tall, solid and old. Its glacial ice is so compacted that the air has been squeezed out, making it ever more blue.

Ice is everywhere here. Our boat's deck is sheathed in a thin layer of it. The boat glances off sizable pieces broken away from the 700,000-square-mile ice pack that surrounds Antarctica each spring.

We've been sailing hard for nearly three full days across the notorious **Drake Passage;** now we're nearing King George Island. It is 75 miles off the tip of the Antarctic continent, in the South Shetland Islands. It's home to a dozen international science bases. And it's where I'd stashed our kayaks during a **recon** trip aboard the *National Geographic Endeavour.*

For the past year I'd started each day punching "polarview.aq" into the nearest computer. (Polar View uses satellite imagery to track sea ice and icebergs in the Antarctic region.) I was trying to get a peek at just how the ice rimming Antarctica was growing or shrinking. Still, we have no idea exactly what conditions we'll find until we drop our kayaks into the ocean. The only sure thing is that the water will be cold—30°F, nearly the freezing point of salt water. The winds will be fierce, building as they race off the sloping plateau out to sea.

Our plan was to get as far south as we could—by kayak, sailboat, and foot—before the ice stopped us. It would amount to one of the most ambitious Antarctic kayaking expeditions in history. (New Zealander and tripmate Graham Charles paddled 528 miles down the coast in 2000.) Along the way we'd meet a handful of scientists and soldiers. We'd get a firsthand assessment of how the rapidly rising temperatures and a related tourism boom are affecting life

> "Ice has a horrible habit of disappearing fast when you get to a critical point, and I think we are at that point now."

at the end of the earth. It's nearly four degrees warmer on the Antarctic Peninsula on average than it was 50 years ago. This is among the more dramatic changes on the planet.

Private expeditions must plan for any emergency. There is no 911 service. No navy. No coast guard. If someone on our team were to break a bone or rupture a spleen, we would have to provide our own ride back to the tip of South America. This explains the *Pelagic Australis*, the 74-foot sailboat I chartered.

We also needed the permission of the U.S. State Department, the National Science Foundation, and the Environmental Protection Agency. The process took more than a year, dozens of lawyer hours, and permits as thick as telephone books. This painstaking pursuit keeps out the daring and unprepared (those who want to bicycle to the South Pole, for example). Ironically, since we planned to camp, we had to fill out more paperwork than the *Star Princess* cruise ship, which carries 3,200 passengers!

For the past decade, each tourist season in Antarctica has set a record. Prices are down. Demand is up. It seems like every tour operator in the world is trying to come here. Permits are required, but the guidelines are unenforceable. Ice-ready boats are also not required.

For now, however, we are alone. I'm standing on the bow of the *Pelagic* on a 20°F morning. I tighten my grasp on a cold metal **stay** as we nudge past a three-foot-thick piece of ice. I'm mindful of the one steadfast rule of sailing in 30°F water: Fall off the boat and you're dead. If you find yourself in the water here, just raise a hand and wave goodbye because the boat will never return fast enough to save you before **hypothermia** sets in.

We take our first paddle strokes on a gray day, about 150 miles down the west coast of the Antarctic Peninsula. We're **circumnavigating** Enterprise Island. I measure the temperature of the ocean—30°F exactly. Air temperatures are in the low 20s. Aside from photographer Pete McBride and videographer John Armstrong, each armed with wet- and drysuits, no one is thinking of going in the water.

LIKE A BIRD
Photographer Pete McBride perches on the ship's boom to take shots of the team as they paddle their kayaks through the Lemaire channel.

We are a group of seven adventurers. Our team includes Chilean mountaineer Rodrigo Jordan, Tasmanian naturalist Fiona Stewart, and California–based navigator Sean Farrell. Armstrong, McBride, Charles, and I make up the rest. We will spend the next few weeks nudging our way southward in custom-built kayaks. The boats are made of carbon fiber, **Kevlar**, and fiberglass. They are reinforced to withstand the ice, and they weigh 700 pounds when fully loaded and manned. Tipping one, and rolling upright again, would be a challenge. If we flipped, we'd have less than five minutes to get out of the water before the cold began to slow our hearts.

For now the sea is calm as we pull around the first corner to find the channel leading out to the Gerlache Strait. This is one of the Antarctic Peninsula's "Kodak Alleys," so called for their typical lineup of picture-perfect bergs. Near shore we thud the boats through thick **brash ice**. It's like paddling in a pool of bucket-size ice cubes.

Each austral winter, a halo of sea ice forms around the continent; each spring trillions of tons of fresh water are released into the ocean as it thaws. This is the beating heart that drives the circulation of Earth's ocean currents. These currents redistribute the sun's heat, regulate climate, and force the upwelling of deep ocean nutrients. They set the tempo of the planet's weather. The Antarctic affects all our lives, but through forces so deep and basic that we're not even aware of them.

Climate change models from the early 1970s predicted that the effects of human greenhouse gas emissions would be felt first and most strongly here. Antarctica is essentially uninhabited and without industry. That means that the ecological and climate disturbances here are caused by global forces. In the 1980s scientists predicted that one of the first signs of human-influenced climate change would be the collapse of the Peninsula's ice sheets. This is exactly what is happening now.

Humans in the Ice Kingdom

As we paddle, our interactions with wildlife are intimate. We often hear the blow of humpback whales breaching before we see them; likewise the plop-plopping of hundreds of penguins leaping from the water as they swim along. We stop and study a half-ton leopard seal floating by on an **ice floe**. He looks at us, belches, then goes back to sleep.

We finish alongside the wreck of the *Guvernoren* in Wilhelmina Bay. This ship was once a floating whale factory. Now only the rusted bow of the ship points out of the calm sea. In the early 21st century, tourism has replaced whaling as Antarctica's boom industry. More than 30 cruise ships, ranging from the hundred-passenger *Endeavour* to the colossal *Star Princess*, visit each season.

But with so many ships, it can be difficult to stay out of each other's way. Expedition leaders now spend much of their time communicating with the surrounding boats, attempting to remain out of sight.

Still, more tourists mean an increased risk of sinkings, fuel spills, and accidents. Last November I was lecturing aboard the *Endeavour* when we came upon the very first tourist ship to sink off Antarctica. Its captain reported hitting ice, which tore through two watertight compartments. Forty-nine thousand gallons of fuel spilled into the ocean. All 154 passengers were safely evacuated that time.

The upside to all these new trips is that more and more visitors are experiencing a conversion of sorts. You cannot take a small boat through one of Antarctica's iceberg alleys without realizing it is the most stunning place on the planet. You cannot stand in the midst of a penguin **rookery**—watching 10,000 of the little creatures file away over the hill in a single line—without smiling. Even the most cynical of tourists simply cannot help but be moved by Antarctica's wonders.

Ten days into our exploration we drag our kayaks onto Petermann Island, where we've spied a big yellow tent. Temperatures have been typical for summer—30s during the day, teens at night.

Calling out, we can hear rustling from inside; researcher Melissa Rider crawls out under a light snowfall. She motions for us to follow her alongside a penguin trail in the snow. This is the fifth summer in a row she's camped on Petermann. Three times a day she counts Adélie and gentoo penguins. On Petermann the results are clear: The Adélies are disappearing.

"Dying?" I ask. "Not necessarily," she says. "They may just be moving farther south. They are cold-loving birds and are having a hard time 'making a living' here, which means building nests, having chicks, and feeding them. . . . What we don't know is where they're going."

"All this warming means that just since last year we've lost 20 percent of the Adélie population on Petermann. If you do the numbers, that means the island will be devoid of them by 2021," Rider says.

ICE GIANT
Near Enterprise Island, Jon Bowermaster and Graham Charles keep a safe distance from a 70-foot iceberg. Icebergs this size have a tendency to roll.

AN UPHILL SLOG
Team members braved the snow to climb Jabed Peak, overlooking Port Lockroy.

WILDLIFE UP CLOSE
This seal allowed a team member to approach for a close-up shot.

Cold Hard Science

The Antarctic Treaty was signed by 12 nations in 1959; it was revised most significantly by 49 countries in 1991. The treaty specifies that Antarctica "is a natural reserve, devoted to peace and science." The treaty specifically bans commercial exploitation until 2041. This refers primarily to the oil and minerals that everyone is certain lie beneath an average of 7,000 feet of ice.

But now those supposedly binding rules are being tested. Most brazenly, last October the United Kingdom announced a new claim to a section nearly the size of Alaska; it overlapped existing claims made by Chile and Argentina. The British government, it seems, hoped to stake out its territory now, before inevitable disputes break out—as they have in the Arctic.

At a few of the bases along the coast we see far more military than scientists. The soldiers represent nations that don't want to relinquish claims to Antarctica but are unwilling to invest in real science programs.

Meanwhile, very real science is still done at the Ukrainian base of Vernadsky. The ozone hole that was growing above Antarctica was discovered at this isolated station in 1984. The ozone layer high above Earth's surface protects people from some of the sun's harmful radiation. The scientists at Verdansky maintain what may be the best meteorological record on the continent; it was started by the British and goes back more than 50 years. The ozone layer was at its thinnest in the mid-1990s; it has begun to fill in during the past decade. In part this is due to the global ban on one class of chemicals.

Where the World Ends

Our camping experience is, in a word, wet, thanks to rain and sleet. Most mornings, the insides of our tent walls are covered with frost; outside, the kayaks anchoring the tents are covered with ice. A few days after paddling away from Vernadsky, the skies clear. And on a sun-filled day, we reach a latitude of nearly 68°S at the southernmost point of Crystal Sound. We are almost two degrees south of the Antarctic Circle, and the temperatures climb into the 40s; sunburn is our biggest concern.

We attempt to thread our way through the two-foot-thick pancake ice before running into a frozen barrier. Through powerful binoculars we see that the two channels we'd hoped to navigate are shut off. Sadly, like every visitor to Antarctica, we've reached our turnaround point.

Having reached our farthest point south, I look back toward the 600 miles we've floated over the past month. Spiky mountain ranges covered with snow lead to glacial skyscrapers running down to the edge of the ocean. I recall a conversation I'd had with Rick Atkinson, caretaker of Port Lockroy, a station that welcomes more than 17,000 tourists a year. Atkinson first came to Antarctica 35 years ago as a dogsled driver and has overseen the renovation of a small museum. Surveying the whiteness around us, I told him I could not imagine this place truly warming, or its ice vanishing anytime soon.

"This rain," he countered, "is the worse thing that can possibly happen. It's a triple whammy: It falls into the **crevasses**, lubricates the bases of glaciers so they move even faster, and it eliminates the insulating layer that keeps the snow solid. Ice has a horrible habit of disappearing fast when you get to a critical point, and I think we are at that point now."

THINK ABOUT IT!

1 **Find Main Ideas and Details** State the article's main point concerning climate change, and give several details that support it.

2 **Make Inferences** What do you think motivated the author to take this trip, and why do you think he chose to go by kayak?

3 **Make Predictions** What do you predict will happen to the tourism business in Antarctica in the near future?

BACKGROUND & VOCABULARY

brash ice *n.* small pieces of floating ice

circumnavigate *v.* (sur-cuhm-NAV-ih-gayt) to sail all the way around a piece of land or the globe

crevasse *n.* (kruh-VAS) a deep crack in thick ice or a glacier

Drake Passage *n.* the strait between South America and the South Shetland Islands

hypothermia *n.* (hy-poh-THUR-mee-uh) a body temperature that is below normal—a potentially life-threatening condition

ice floe *n.* a large, flat piece of floating ice

Kevlar *n.* (KEHV-lahr) a very strong fiber used for protective vests

recon *n.* (REE-kawn) an earlier exploration or inspection (short for *reconnaissance*)

rookery *n.* (ROO-kuhr-ee) a breeding ground of penguins or certain other sea birds

stay *n.* a cable supporting a mast on a sailing boat

CREEPING DANGER
A brinicle descends from surface ice near Antarctica's Little Razorback Island, freezing sea stars and urchins as it advances.

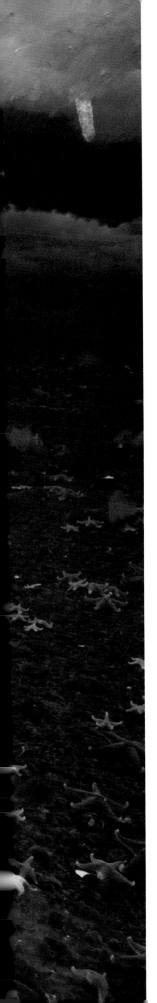

The Brinicle

BY JEREMY BERLIN

Adapted from "Ice Stalactites," by Jeremy Berlin, in *National Geographic*, May 2012

In the frigid waters of Antarctica, **briny** tubes of ice can stretch down to the sea floor.

Oddities abound at the world's poles. Now, thanks to time-lapse cameras, we can see one coming to life. This salty ice **stalactite**, called a brinicle, was filmed as it formed by British cameramen Doug Anderson and Hugh Miller in Antarctica's McMurdo Sound.

Ice stalactites were first described in detail in 1971 by American oceanographers Paul Dayton and Seelye Martin. Martin actually grew them in his Seattle laboratory. According to him, brinicles occur naturally in polar winters. Conditions are right there because air temperatures can dip well below 0°F, while the water may be a relatively balmy 28°F.

The difference between the water and air temperatures is key. The phenomenon involves relatively warm sea water rising, cooling, and dropping again. The sea ice on the surface is filled with a network of channels. When the warmer seawater rises upward, it flows into these channels in the sea ice. The water cools. The dense brine in the sea water is too salty to become part of the ice pack. Instead, it drains out and sinks back into the ocean. As it descends, the brine freezes the water around it. This forms a plume that grows downward at about one foot an hour. If conditions are just right, a brinicle can reach the seabed. There it creeps along the bottom, pooling at low points.

In the 1970s, Martin recalls with a laugh that "the Navy asked if they're dangerous to submarines." They're not. In fact, brinicles are too slow forming to freeze anything but bottom dwellers such as sea stars. And they're fragile enough to be broken apart by seals or currents. When that occurs, or when the brine stops seeping, a brinicle "dies." But it may get a second life. Anderson has seen fish making homes of dead brinicles covered in **platelet ice**. Platelet ice forms structures resembling "very beautiful chandeliers"—just another polar curiosity.

THINK ABOUT IT! |||||||||||

Make Inferences Why is the brinicle deadly to sea stars but not to fish?

BACKGROUND & VOCABULARY

briny *adj.* (BRY-nee) containing a large amount of salt, or saturated with salt

platelet ice *n.* (PLAYT-liht) the ice crystals typical of Antarctica that form in supercooled water under certain conditions

stalactite *n.* (stuh-LAHK-tyt) a mineral deposit shaped like an icicle, typically hanging from the roof of a cave

Whales *of the* Antarctic

At least a dozen species of whales live in Antarctic waters year-round or part-time. Some feed on a tiny shrimplike organism called krill; others go after larger prey. All are key parts of the Antarctic ecosystem.

CATCHING SOME AIR
Near the Antarctic shore, a humpback whale breaches—leaps from the water, spins in the air, and splashes down on its side. Scientists do not know for sure why humpbacks breach, but the behavior may be a way to communicate with other whales.

WHALES OF ALL SIZES

The Antarctic waters are home to an astounding variety of whale species.

Southern Right Whale

Human

Humpback Whale

Killer Whale or Orca

Southern Bottlenose Whale

Arnoux's Beaked Whale

Strap-toothed Beaked Whale

Hourglass Dolphin

Spectacled Porpoise

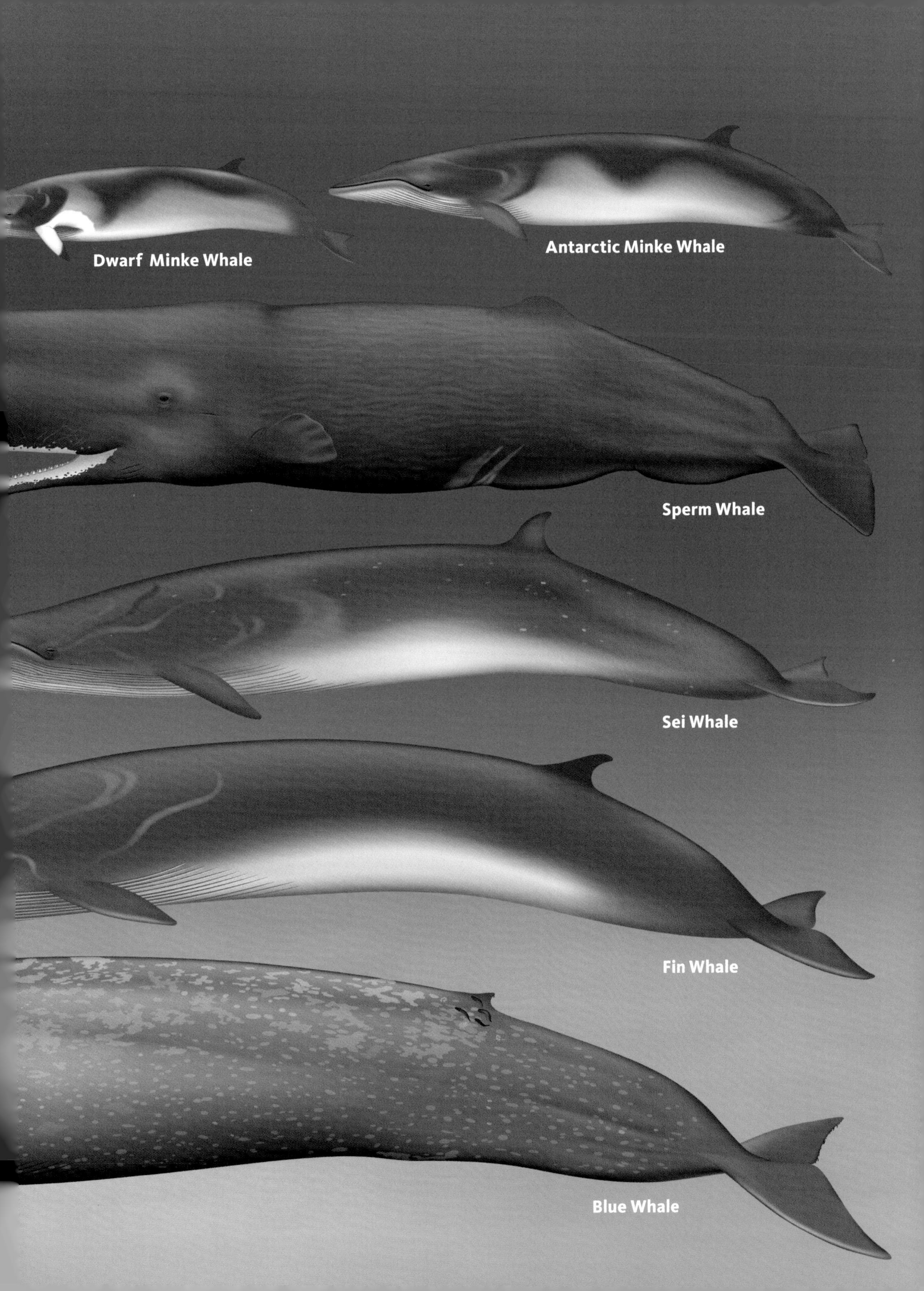

Dwarf Minke Whale

Antarctic Minke Whale

Sperm Whale

Sei Whale

Fin Whale

Blue Whale

"... I thought to myself, this is how whales behave with humans when they've had no bad experiences. This is how it was meant to be."

—Brian Skerry, National Geographic Photographer

GENTLE GIANT
National Geographic Photographer Brian Skerry captured amazing shots of this 45-foot-long, 70-ton southern right whale off the coast of New Zealand. Skerry took photographs in rapid succession while directing his assistant Mauricio Handler into the best position for the shot. The whale was not afraid of the men and stayed around for two hours, allowing them to photograph it.

THINK ABOUT IT! ||||||||||||||||||||||||||||||||||

Analyze Visuals What skills do you think you would have to have as a photographer to be able to capture this photograph?

Frozen**Under**

BY ROFF SMITH
Adapted from "Frozen Under," by Roff Smith, in *National Geographic*, December 2001

FROZEN BEAUTY
Mount Erebus looms in the distance as ice floes bob on the surface of McMurdo Sound.

Antarctica offers opportunities for scientists to learn what Earth was like millions of years ago, how different forces affect the planet today, and what changes may come in the future. Here, writer Roff Smith writes about his trip to Antarctica to meet some of the people working to discover its secrets.

Volcanic Mount Erebus rises nearly two and a half miles above the Ross Sea off the coast of East Antarctica. As I approached the crater, Rick Aster called out to me, "Don't try to run if it erupts. Just stand still, look up, and be ready to step aside if anything comes your way. This thing can throw lava bombs the size of a sofa." I peered over the rim into a smoky chasm 2,000 feet across and more than 700 feet deep. At the bottom of the pit, beneath swirling smoke, lay a pool of lava.

"That lava has been bubbling for decades, perhaps centuries," explained Aster. "You are looking at one of the few permanent lava lakes in the world—a living window into what goes on miles below the Earth's surface." Aster is a geophysicist from the New Mexico Institute of Mining and Technology. Geophysicists use geology, physics, and mathematics to study Earth.

Antarctica offers scientists unique views of Earth's workings. These include active volcanoes, fast-flowing glaciers, and unstable ice sheets that slide unstoppably to the coast. Some of the world's most violent storms and mountainous seas batter the lonely islands off the Antarctic Peninsula. The interior is a sterile void, where temperatures plunge to -120°F. Yet the frigid waters that surround the continent are among the world's richest and most biologically diverse. Antarctica influences weather patterns across the Southern Hemisphere. It shapes ocean currents throughout the world. And it reflects an eye-opening picture of human use and abuse of the planet.

For all its distance, Antarctica is accessible now as never before. More than 250 flights land at the South Pole each summer. Cruise ships bring more than 12,000 tourists every year. The numbers keep growing. McMurdo Station is the local headquarters of the National Science Foundation, which operates the U.S. Antarctic Program. It is the largest settlement on the continent. McMurdo has a summertime population of about 1,100. It has a busy airport, ATMs, speed-limit signs, and a shuttle bus that takes riders to New Zealand's Scott Base, two miles away.

HEAT AND ICE
Hot gases and vapor escape from vents near
the ice-wreathed peak of Mount Erebus.

Nobody owns Antarctica. Earth's fifth largest continent has been set aside as a natural reserve devoted to peace and science since the signing of the 1959 Antarctic Treaty. (Protection was extended to the surrounding oceans in 1982.) The treaty's signers represent more than half the human population. "Scientists and universities that would be competitors in the real world [work together] here," says Chris Martin of the Harvard-Smithsonian Center for Astrophysics.

The cooperation promotes science. It also preserves Antarctica's considerable resources. Geologists already know there are coal seams in the Transantarctic Mountains. Traces of gold, platinum, and copper have been found scattered around the continent. But at an international conference in 1991, treaty nations agreed to ban attempts at mining until at least 2041. For now science will be Antarctica's major industry.

Science in Antarctica

One morning I was flown by helicopter to Darwin Glacier. We were on our way to a field camp in the Transantarctic Mountains, about 180 miles south of McMurdo. There, geologists were looking back 270 million years to a time when Antarctica was a wilderness of forests, **tundra**, and marsh. It was part of a giant continent known as **Gondwana**.

Antarctica may be drier than the Sahara and as cold as Mars. It is nearly as lifeless. However, it wasn't always like this. "The scenery would have resembled parts of Alaska perhaps, with a few large glaciers around," said Rosemary Askin, a paleontologist with Ohio State University's Byrd Polar Research Center. Paleontologists study fossils to learn about Earth's history.

The next morning found us about 8,500 feet up a splintery tower of rock and ice called Mount

bubbles to compare them with samples of today's atmosphere. This lets them follow the course of Earth's climate through the past 420,000 years. They can spot the sharp rise in greenhouse gases that is associated with our burning of fossil fuels.

Antarctica is also where human-made pollutants called chlorofluorocarbons end up. For a long time, we used these compounds in aerosols and coolants. Winds carry these chemicals south. There they mix with high-altitude clouds in the cold and dark of Antarctica's winter. As the sun returns in spring, the frozen chemical clouds react with its rays. They release chlorine molecules that temporarily dissolve the thin layer of ozone that protects life on Earth from harmful solar radiation. The hole in the ozone layer was first noted in 1985 by three British scientists working in Antarctica. It reappears each spring.

Next in my Antarctic travels, I boarded a ski-equipped cargo plane bound for the South Pole. All my fellow passengers were astrophysicists— astronomers who study the physical aspects of objects in space. A three-hour flight brought us to the ice runway at the Amundsen-Scott South Pole Station. We scrambled out of the hatch, blinking in the polar glare. It was a perfect summer day. The temperature stood at -28°F, the windchill at -54°F, and a double halo of ice crystals circled the bright sun.

"It's the next best thing to being there," says Jeffery Peterson, an astrophysicist from Carnegie Mellon University. Peterson is talking about Antarctica's hostile, spacelike conditions. Peterson is chief scientist for the high-resolution Viper radio telescope. He continues, "Viewing conditions here are nearly as good as for the **Hubble Space Telescope**. We are almost 10,000 feet high and hundreds of miles from the ocean. There is virtually no water vapor in the air, the sky is transparent, and the atmosphere is extremely stable. This [environment] is a perfect window to the universe."

Next I headed south aboard a ship chartered by the U.S. Antarctic Marine Living Resources program. Its crew of scientists was beginning a three-month survey of the Scotia Sea and the coastal waters off the South Shetland Islands. This survey was part of an ongoing study of Antarctica's marine ecosystem.

Henderson. It was a beautiful summer day. The temperature was a balmy 38°F without a breath of wind. Chips of petrified wood as crisp as freshly cut timber lay scattered under our boots. We were at least 2,000 miles from the nearest living tree.

"This is probably *Glossopteris* wood," Askin explained, as she handed me the stump of an ancient sapling. "It was a . . . tree that also lived in South America, Africa, India, and Australia. Finding it in Antarctica was one of the things that proved the continents must have been linked at one time."

Scientists who study ice and how it affects the planet find an equally well-preserved record in Antarctica. More than 99 percent of the continent is covered by ice in massive beds up to 15,600 feet thick. They are the result of a slow but steady build-up of snowfall over time. Gas bubbles sealed in the ice act as time capsules. Researchers drill **ice cores** and analyze the

ICEBERG PASSENGERS
A group of chinstrap penguins hitches a ride on an eroded iceberg. These penguins must swim ever farther from land in search of krill to eat.

"That ultimately means krill," said Roger Hewitt, the expedition leader. Krill are the tiny shrimplike animals that swarm in Antarctica's seas. "Everything eats them," Hewitt went on, "from hundred-ton blue whales to seals and penguins, birds and fish, right on down to the tiny **zooplankton** that feed on krill larvae."

Humans too. Factory ships take about 100,000 tons of krill each year. Krill are processed into krill oil capsules that provide omega-3 fatty acids. These ships also take thousands of tons of fish such as Patagonian toothfish and Antarctic cod. In an attempt to manage the rich fisheries in Antarctica's waters, the Antarctic Treaty nations formed the Convention for the Conservation of Antarctic Marine Living Resources in 1982. Hewitt and his crew were studying marine life in support of the convention's mission. I asked Hewitt whether commercial fishing could be causing problems. "We are not as concerned about the quantity of krill being harvested," he explained, "as we are about where and when it is being caught."

Krill live along submerged shelves and off points of land. There they are convenient pickings for land-based predators such as seals and penguins. Those animals establish breeding colonies nearby. "These same easy pickings draw the fishing fleets," Hewitt explained. "[Nearly] all krill fishing is done within 50 miles of these colonies, so while 100,000 tons isn't much in terms of overall krill **biomass**, it may represent a large portion of the wildlife's food source."

Scientists are also studying how climate change might affect krill. "We suspect that warmer winters may be having an impact on krill's ability to breed successfully," said Valerie Loeb, an oceanographer at California State University. "Krill feed on algae that grow on the bottom of winter sea ice, but cold winters with extensive sea ice are becoming less frequent. The last successful breeding year for krill was 1995."

I arranged to join up with a team of researchers on Livingston Island. They study krill from a predator's viewpoint. I met Wayne Trivelpiece, who studies seabirds. "I've been coming down here every summer for the past 25 years," he said. He led me along the coast. It was covered with thousands of fur seals and dotted with the nests of 7,700 breeding pairs of chinstrap penguins.

By monitoring penguin and fur seal colonies, we can get a pretty accurate idea of how healthy krill stocks are," Trivelpiece said. "During the past ten years we have seen a sharp decline in the survival rate of penguin chicks. Their parents are doing quite well . . . but the naive chicks are just not surviving those first . . . weeks of foraging on their own. With so few krill close by, they have to swim out farther and longer in search of food."

Equally worrying is the lack of young krill showing up in the penguins' diets. This indicates the krill themselves are not breeding successfully. "Looking over meteorological records going back to 1903, we are seeing a gradual warming trend here since the 1940s," Trivelpiece said. ". . . Satellite images also record a pronounced change in the cycle of winter sea ice since about 1970. Instead of consistently extensive winter pack we are now getting maybe two good years followed by up to five warm, ice-free winters. No ice means no food for the young krill. What we are seeing here is the first evidence of how a shift in climate may have a surprisingly quick and dramatic impact."

Living in Antarctica

I left Livingston Island on a 65-foot yacht skippered by French explorer, scientist, and writer, Jérôme Poncet. We arrived late in the evening two days later at King George Island, also in the South Shetlands. Maxwell Bay is a picture-postcard scene surrounded by glaciers and mountains on the southern tip of the island. The lights of scattered bases twinkled along the shore. King George Island is a melting pot where Argentina, Brazil, Chile, China, Poland, Russia, South Korea, and Uruguay all maintain year-round bases. Other nations, including the United States, Ecuador, Peru, Germany, Netherlands, and the Czech Republic, operate summer camps here as well.

There is a reason this 500-square-mile island is the trendiest real estate in Antarctica. King George Island lies only 600 miles from South America and has a 4,400-foot airstrip to provide quick access. Under the terms of the Antarctic Treaty, only nations conducting scientific research in Antarctica have a voice in shaping the continent's future. Setting up a base on King George Island is the simplest way to get that voice.

While environmentalists dislike the extra bases crowded on the island, others see the settlement as a unique international community. "Here we have a beginning, a light," says Sergio Lizasoain, chief of operations for Chile's Antarctic program. He first came to Antarctica in 1957. He remarks, "Look around you. On this little island we have people from all over the world living in harmony with each other. There are no borders, no passports, no politics."

THINK ABOUT IT! ||||||||||||||||||||||||||||||||

1 **Find Main Ideas and Details** What types of scientific activity take place in Antarctica, and why is Antarctica a good place to pursue them?

2 **Summarize** How does the article describe how people feel about living in Antarctica?

3 **Analyze Cause and Effect** What causes and effects of climate change does the writer describe in the article?

BACKGROUND & VOCABULARY

biomass *n.* (BY-oh-mas) the living matter in an area or a population

Gondwana *n.* (gahnd-WAH-nuh) a supercontinent fully formed about 600 million years ago that included today's South America, Africa, Arabia, Madagascar, India, Australia, and Antarctica

Hubble Space Telescope *n.* (HUHB-uhl) a telescope that orbits outside of Earth's atmosphere

ice core *n.* a tubular sample drilled out of deep ice

tundra *n.* (TUHN-druh) a treeless plain with a permanently frozen deeper layer of soil

zooplankton *n.* (zoh-uh-PLANGK-tuhn) the animals among the very small organisms that float in water and serve as food for larger organisms

Document-Based Question

The southern continent has always held a place in the popular imagination. Long before the first humans set foot on Antarctica, dreamers and explorers imagined that there was land at the South Pole. Since that time, scientists working there have revealed Antarctica bit by bit, although it still guards some mysteries. As our knowledge evolves, so does our understanding of the world around us.

DOCUMENT 1 Secondary Source

Methane in Antarctic Ice

In 2012, National Geographic's *Daily News* website reported a discovery by scientists in the Antarctic. It linked the prehistoric time when Antarctica had a temperate climate to today's concerns about climate change. Methane, produced from the remains of ancient organisms by bacteria hidden in the ice, contributes to global warming today.

Swamp gas trapped under miles of Antarctic ice, a chemical souvenir of that continent's warmer days, may someday escape to warm the planet again, an international team of researchers report. The researchers suggest that microbes isolated from the rest of the world since the ice closed over them, some 35 million years ago, have kept busy digesting organic matter and making methane [a greenhouse gas]. If global warming causes the ice sheets to retreat in the coming decades or centuries, the researchers warn, some of the methane could belch into the atmosphere, [increasing] the warming.

from "Antarctic Methane Could Escape, Worsen Warming," by Rob Kunzig, news.nationalgeographic.com, August 31, 2012

CONSTRUCTED RESPONSE

1. What is the origin of the methane trapped beneath Antarctic ice sheets, and what might happen to release it into the atmosphere?

DOCUMENT 2 Primary Source

Aboard a Research Cruise

In 2013, Cassandra Brooks, a Stanford University graduate student, joined a National Science Foundation research cruise in the Ross Sea in Antarctica. She shared her experiences via a blog she wrote while on assignment.

We've sampled more than 100 different locations in the Ross Sea and my hands are cracked, chapped, and leather-like from long days working with the cold and salty water. The temperatures outside have dipped below zero degrees, dropping to -60°F with the wind chill, and the sea continues to ice over. Some of our equipment is beginning to freeze. Perhaps the idea of working thousands of miles from home in one of the coldest environments on Earth sounds miserable . . . But while I miss having fresh fruits and vegetables to eat, I am hardly suffering . . . . Our vessel has the finest at-sea working and living conditions I've yet encountered. Further, we are outfitted . . . with extreme cold weather gear that keeps us warm even if we have to work outside in the -60°F.

from "Fighting for the Last Tomato: Surviving a Field Season in Antarctica," by Cassandra Brooks, newswatch.nationalgeographic.com, March 12, 2013

CONSTRUCTED RESPONSE

2. What kinds of challenges does Brooks encounter while researching and living aboard the ship in the Ross Sea?

What can we learn about our world from research in **Antarctica?**

DOCUMENT 3 Primary Source
International Continent

This present-day map of Antarctica shows the continent, the surrounding oceans, and the locations of international research stations. It also shows international boundaries of several countries. The colored lines mark the boundaries of international claims.

CONSTRUCTED RESPONSE

3. In what ways does this map illustrate international cooperation in Antarctica?

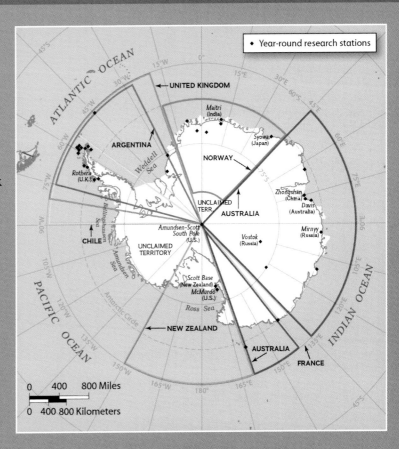

PUT IT TOGETHER ||||||||||||||||||||||||||||||||||||||||||||||||||||||||||||||||||||||||||||||||||||||||||

Review Think about your responses to the Constructed Response questions here and what you have learned about Antarctica from the articles in this book.

Summarize Review the primary and secondary sources on this page. In a sentence, summarize each source. Consider what the sources have in common with each other.

Write Write a topic sentence that answers this question: What can we learn about our world from research in Antarctica? Then write a paragraph that supports your topic sentence using evidence from the documents.

INDEX

|||||||||||||||||||||||||||||||||||||||||||||||||||||

SKILLS